THE POETRY BUS

A Treasure Trove Of Rhyme

Edited By Lynsey Evans

First published in Great Britain in 2024 by:

Young Writers
Remus House
Coltsfoot Drive
Peterborough
PE2 9BF
Telephone: 01733 890066
Website: www.youngwriters.co.uk

All Rights Reserved
Book Design by Ashley Janson
© Copyright Contributors 2024
Softback ISBN 978-1-83565-541-2
Printed and bound in the UK by BookPrintingUK
Website: www.bookprintinguk.com
YB0594T

FOREWORD

Welcome to a fun-filled book of poems!

Here at Young Writers we are delighted to introduce The Poetry Bus. Pupils could choose to write an acrostic, sense poem or riddle to introduce them to the world of poetry. Giving them this framework allowed the young writers to open their imaginations to a range of topics of their choice, and encouraged them to include other poetic techniques such as similes and descriptive vocabulary.

From family and friends, to animals and places, these pupils have shaped and crafted their ideas brilliantly, showcasing their budding creativity in verse.

We live and breathe creativity here at Young Writers – it gives us life! We want to pass our love of the written word onto the next generation and what better way to do that than to celebrate their writing by publishing it in a book!

Each awesome little poet in this book should be super proud of themselves! We hope you will delight in these poems as much as we have.

CONTENTS

Ardeley St Lawrence CE (VA) Primary School, Ardeley

Darcy Jenkins (6)	1
Ruby Milton (7)	2
Jacob Crossman (7)	3
Aurora Baker (5)	4
Jude Martin (6)	5
Charlie Heuer (6)	6

Bute House Preparatory School, Hammersmith

Constance Yang-Feng (4)	7
Elektra Folkerts (4)	8
Alisha Subramanyam (5)	9
Yizhen Xu (5)	10
Rose Han (4)	11
Junyi Jiang (5)	12
Lana Al-Uzri (5)	13
Emma Wang (5)	14
Lia Hasan (5)	15

Central Park Primary School, London

Zainab Hafizi (7)	16
Noah Chaudhary (7)	17
Amal Qabaha (6)	18
Asiya Bharodawala (6)	19
Aaminah Ahmed (7)	20
Ava Mizan (7)	21
Giullia Maria Alexe (7)	22
Jasmeen Kaur (5)	23
Safa Ali (6)	24
Musfira Ahmed (6)	25

Abida Siddika (6)	26
Eesa Shehzad (6)	27
Tiamadu Ava Magia (6)	28
Tasnim Hussain (6)	29
Arissa Quddus (7)	30
Zahin Raia (7)	31
Sarim Ali (6)	32
Ayesha Khan (6)	33
Kamila Hussain (6)	34
Ayris Hossain (6)	35
Iliya Minhas (7)	36
Rayah Rayah (7)	37
Sarah Yasmin (6)	38
Anayah Arif (7)	39
Mukarram Ali Shan (6)	40
Zarah Zeeshan (7)	41
Saad Javed (6)	42
Arya Choudhury (6)	43
Jasleen Singh Tena (7)	44
Karina Croitoriu (6)	45
Halima Alam (7)	46
Khadijah Sultan (6)	47
Qaasim Desai (7)	48
Idris Raja Ali (4)	49
Syed Muhammad Mudassir Shah (6)	50

Downshall Primary School, Seven Kings

Klyan Afrose (6)	51
Nimrit Kaur (5)	52
Maryam Aidha (5)	53
Ahmad Patel (6)	54
Yahya Santally (5)	55
Imaani Ahmed (5)	56

Yafiah Adeel (6)	57
Salaar Tayub (6)	58
Nuh Valli (5)	59
Miguel Omieczynska-Sipi (6)	60
Pranavi Vengatesan (6)	61

Edgebury Primary School, Chislehurst

Harrison Pasfield (5)	62
Ada Harrison (5)	64
Harleen Kaur Blaggan (5)	65
Alice Fairhurst-Stanier (4)	66
Ryan Khosoroshahy (7)	67
Violet Wilcox (7)	68
Jinay Godha (7)	69
Tomás Da Costa Fonseca (6)	70
Ted Power (6)	71
Leila Mustafaj (6)	72
Poppy Williams (6)	73
Tilly Cheeseman (7)	74
Finlay Smith (7)	75
Olive Alcock (6)	76
Alex Lintern (6)	77
Nason Taylor-Holmes (7)	78
Lucas Halley (6)	79
Milan D'Rozario (5)	80
Lydia Mathieson (4)	81
Louis Burtt (7)	82
Senan Harris (6)	83
George Celaschi (6)	84
Melisa Mehmet (7)	85
Jaxon Davis (5)	86
Nora Marini (7)	87
Maddie Sharps (7)	88
Bethany Da Silva (7)	89
Jacob Borg (6)	90
Alex Foster (4)	91
Leo Gooding (7)	92
Isabelle Naden (6)	93
Emelia Harris (6)	94
Ophelia Nelson (5)	95
Joshua Banis (6)	96
Annie Manning (6)	97

Alisa Bejan (5)	98
Nina Vaccarino (6)	99
Emre Azmi (6)	100
Austin Haines (6)	101
Amanie Clement (6)	102
Halle Exford Downes (7)	103
Chester Ramsden (6)	104
Neli Roslaniec (4)	105
Saraya Matharu (7)	106
Noelle De Chavez (5)	107
Freja Warren (4)	108
Giuseppe Noto (6)	109
Zara Hersey-Walker (6)	110
James Munro (5)	111
Lily-Grace Eaves (5)	112
Zac Kenny (6)	113
Cyrus Phan (6)	114
Luca Wall (5)	115
Iris Haines (4)	116
Desara Brahaj (6)	117
Esme Pfeiffer (6)	118
Arian Jeddi (6)	119
Olivia Rorison-Warburton (6)	120
Emily Watts Stropute (5)	121
Liam Carta (6)	122
Cody Carey (7)	123
Freya Putz (5)	124
George Pinker (6)	125
Lyla Jaques (7)	126
Dealarra Ezzra Muhd Azrainuddin (6)	127
Zahara Okasha (6)	128
Ari Aubeeluck (5)	129
Eliza Gregoriou (6)	130
Ela Nacar (6)	131
Sidney Hayes (6)	132
Anthony Woodward (4)	133
Amos Reynolds (5)	134
Quincy Rawlings (5)	135
Amelia Reid (4)	136
Eldridge Ofori-Boakye (6)	137
Finn Thomas (5)	138
Freddie Dykes (4)	139

Finley Borg (4)	140
Jake Manning (4)	141
Lum Iberhasaj (6)	142
Joseph Clement (4)	143
Leila Francis (5)	144
Ronnie Whitlock (5)	145
Archie Whitlock (4)	146
Jacob Rudnicki (5)	147
Mila Xhetani (7)	148
Isla Turner (4)	149

THE POEMS

My Spring Sense Poem

I can see baby animals being born.
I can hear birds tweeting in the trees.
I can touch the beautiful flowers.
I can smell fresh bark on the trees.
I can taste yummy ice cream that gives me blue teeth.

Darcy Jenkins (6)
Ardeley St Lawrence CE (VA) Primary School, Ardeley

My Spring Sense Poem

I can see lovely flowers bloom
I can hear birds tweeting in the trees
I can touch the cold ice
I can smell fresh bark on the tree
I can taste yummy picnics.

Ruby Milton (7)
Ardeley St Lawrence CE (VA) Primary School, Ardeley

My Spring Senses Poem

I can see the baby dogs
I can hear the lambs bleating
I can feel the cold on my face
I can smell the beautiful flowers
I can taste Easter eggs.

Jacob Crossman (7)
Ardeley St Lawrence CE (VA) Primary School, Ardeley

My Spring Sense Poem

I can see some snow.
I can hear the wind.
I can feel my soft, wild rabbit.
I can smell the flowers.
I can taste Easter eggs.

Aurora Baker (5)
Ardeley St Lawrence CE (VA) Primary School, Ardeley

My Poem Is About...

I can see the Easter bunny,
I can hear birds tweet,
I can feel my skin,
I can smell blue flowers,
I can taste Easter eggs.

Jude Martin (6)
Ardeley St Lawrence CE (VA) Primary School, Ardeley

My Spring Sense Poem

I can see fresh bark
I can smell fresh apples
I can feel leaves
I can hear llamas
I can taste apples.

Charlie Heuer (6)
Ardeley St Lawrence CE (VA) Primary School, Ardeley

This Is Me

C ats are my favourite pets
O ranges are my favourite fruit
N ame a fruit you like
S tring snacks are fun
T eddies are lovely toys
A nd I like ants
N athan is my love
C akes are what I love
E xiting, what do you like?

Constance Yang-Feng (4)
Bute House Preparatory School, Hammersmith

All About Me

E verything used as a stick
L ovely and caring
E xciting books I like
K oalas are my favourite
T rees are my favourite
R eading is what I like
A nd what do you like?

Elektra Folkerts (4)
Bute House Preparatory School, Hammersmith

All About Me

A mazing knowledge I have
L ovely llamas are cute
I love sour lollipops
S plitting on the slide is my favourite
H ousework is fun to me
A nd how about you?

Alisha Subramanyam (5)
Bute House Preparatory School, Hammersmith

Yizhen

Y ellow is my favourite colour
I like skipping
Z ebras are my favourite animal
H opping is lovely
E lephants are giant
k **N** itting is very fun.

Yizhen Xu (5)
Bute House Preparatory School, Hammersmith

All About Me

w **R** apping presents is my favourite sound,
   O reos and orange juice is what I like to eat and drink,
   S wimming is what I love,
   E lephant is my favourite animal.

Rose Han (4)
Bute House Preparatory School, Hammersmith

Junyi

J umping on the trampoline
U nicorns are nice
N ame wonderful
Y ellow's my favourite colour
I like a yo-yo.

Junyi Jiang (5)
Bute House Preparatory School, Hammersmith

Lana

L ana is lovely and nice
A urélia is my best friend
k **N** itting is fun
A pple is my favourite fruit.

Lana Al-Uzri (5)
Bute House Preparatory School, Hammersmith

My Favourite Things

E ggs are not my favourite,
M onkeys are funny,
M asks are what I like,
A pples are my favourite fruit.

Emma Wang (5)
Bute House Preparatory School, Hammersmith

Poem About Lia

L ia is lovely and funny
I like delicious Oreos
A pple is my favourite fruit.

Lia Hasan (5)
Bute House Preparatory School, Hammersmith

Mother Nature Forever

From farms to barns
Flowers, to nature's superpowers
We could all live a happy life if the world was kept clean
For example, if the environment was gleaming with green
The world can't be filled with flowing streams here, and a bunch of bears there
We all have to take part and do our fair share
Do not litter
Or the world will be bitter
Give your car a rest
Instead, take a few steps
This will not just affect me or you
It will help everyone if you do!

Zainab Hafizi (7)
Central Park Primary School, London

Football

F ootball is my all-time favourite game
O llie Watkins, Ronaldo, Messi and Mbappé are famous players' names
"**O** ffside, foul, penalty!" the referee shouts
T ackles, drills and throw-ins
B eing the best takes a lot of getting hurt
A ll the players celebrate by taking off their shirts
L iverpool has Trent, Arsenal has Saka and Man U has Mason Mount
L ittle League, Premier League. It all counts.

Noah Chaudhary (7)
Central Park Primary School, London

The Helpful Cat

H ideous cat which tells jokes
E ating his supper peacefully
L ikes to tell people the right things
P lays with others so they can feel happy
F luffy toys he likes, he likes
U pside-down offices
He **L** ikes football at a beach. He likes

C arnivals so he can see the acrobats, he likes
A sunny day and to go to the beach
T iring days he does not like very much.

Amal Qabaha (6)
Central Park Primary School, London

What We Can Be

R espectful is what we should be
E veryone should have some honesty
S haring is what we all need
P eople shouldn't be that mean
E ven when we disagree
C ourtesy is the best policy
T he best that you will ever be
F un and joy, all positivity
U nfriendly is what we should never be
L ive and love, life is a special cup of tea.

Asiya Bharodawala (6)
Central Park Primary School, London

The Night Cat

I am a black cat,
I blend into the night sky,
But I know the places to hide,
Climbing trees is my favourite hobby,
I don't like to be sloppy,
Climbing trees is my favourite thing to do,
So I can have a very high view,
Hopping on buildings is fun too,
It makes everyone think I'm a mysterious cat,
But everyone loves the way I play,
In the night, at the end of the day.

Aaminah Ahmed (7)
Central Park Primary School, London

Ramadan

R amadan is when Muslims fast for a month.
A ll Muslims stop eating and drinking from sunrise to sunset.
M uslims break their fast with a meal called iftar.
A ll Muslims read the Quran and pray together.
D onating to charity helps poor people in Ramadan.
A t the end of Ramadan, Muslims celebrate Eid
N ew presents are shared during Ramadan and Eid.

Ava Mizan (7)
Central Park Primary School, London

Butterfly

B utterflies are so beautiful
U nique wings
T ickles your hands
T hey all have different colours
E ach time it grows
R ainbow colours
F lower nectar
L ike a butterfly
I like butterflies
E very butterfly is special
S o butterflies are so pretty.

Giullia Maria Alexe (7)
Central Park Primary School, London

A Kid's Journey Of Delight

Salty popcorn tickles my nose,
Bright colours of candy,
My eyes do behold,
Soft cotton candy melts on my tongue,
Bumpy roller coasters make my body feel young,
Giggles and laughter fill the air,
The smell of fresh rain,
After a not-sunny day,
All these sensations make childhood play.

Jasmeen Kaur (5)
Central Park Primary School, London

My Senses

Glow the bright sun, the blue sky,
I can see the white snow, I can see you!
I can smell the roast meat, the fresh bread, the pretty flowers,
I can smell your dirty feet, I can smell you!
I can touch the soft grass, the cold ice, the wet rain,
I can touch the smooth glass, I can touch you!

Safa Ali (6)
Central Park Primary School, London

The Four Seasons

S pring is the first season,
E njoy a new beginning and hope,
A nd then we have summer,
S ummer is sunny and fun,
O ver the moon when leaves change colour in autumn,
N ext is winter, the coldest of them all,
S mile and enjoy all the seasons!

Musfira Ahmed (6)
Central Park Primary School, London

Guess The Celebration

I bring smiles, I bring cheer,
A special day that's very near,
New clothes we wear, delicious treats we eat,
After Ramadan I take a seat,
To Nana's house, we visit every year,
A celebration for you and me,
With family and friends,
What am I?
It's pure delight.

Abida Siddika (6)
Central Park Primary School, London

Football

I love football,
I enjoy dribbling the ball,
I have skills,
That make the referee get chills,
I score a goal from far away,
Which has the goalkeeper in dismay,
I celebrate in style,
Which makes the crowd smile,
This is why I love football,
Because it's so cool.

Eesa Shehzad (6)
Central Park Primary School, London

Running

Running is fun.
I run a lot in school.
In the winter, it's cold and I can't run a lot.
Running is healthy for people.
It is also for warming up.
Running is exercise, nothing can stop running.
Running is not only running, it is a race.
We run to find peace.

Tiamadu Ava Magia (6)
Central Park Primary School, London

My Lockdown Acrostic Poem

L ockdown is sad because I miss my friends.
O ut in the garden is lots of fun.
C ooking our pizzas.
K eeping safe.
D on't go outside.
O n lots of fun bike rides.
W alks in the forest.
N obody can go to school.

Tasnim Hussain (6)
Central Park Primary School, London

My Mummy Rose

My mummy loves roses,
She always smells like rose petals,
When she sees roses, she turns into a red rose,
Red is her favourite colour,
My mummy loves to grow roses,
But she cries when they die,
I love you, Mummy Rose,
As you are my beautiful rose.

Arissa Quddus (7)
Central Park Primary School, London

Rainbow

R ainbows make you happy
A lways make you smile
I love to see a rainbow
N ow a rainbow makes you run a mile
B ecause a rainbow is colourful
O ur rainbow will shine for you
W ould I love to see another one?

Zahin Raia (7)
Central Park Primary School, London

Football

F ootball is fun,
O ut in the sun.
O ut in the rain,
T o give me pain.
B alls are my friend,
A re they in my favourite sport? Oh, yes.
L oved it all my life,
L oved by the crowds.

Sarim Ali (6)
Central Park Primary School, London

How I Can Be

A fter a long time at school,
Y ou might wonder what I do to be cool,
E very day I try to be fast,
S ometimes unfortunately I'm last,
H owever, I don't mind,
A fter all, I am still always kind!

Ayesha Khan (6)
Central Park Primary School, London

A Chicken Leg Got Snipped By A Hairy Peg

So once there was a chicken leg
Who hated hairy pegs
For he was a small piece of chicken leg
So one day he was naughty and finally got pegged
For little chicken leg was always scared
And he was not naughty again
He was forlorn.

Kamila Hussain (6)
Central Park Primary School, London

Sense Poem - The Mango

In the summer holidays, I sit next to the tree,
Something smells,
Something sweet and sugary,
Looks yellow and yum,
It's shiny!
It's a mango!
Buzzy bees buzzing around the yellow mango,
I love yellow mangoes.

Ayris Hossain (6)
Central Park Primary School, London

A Mother's Love

My mum has a day full of love.
Her favourite bird is a dove.
My mum is nice.
She likes ice.
My mum is as fine
As sun can shine.
The sky is blue and the grass is green.
Everyone wants to be on Mummy's team.

Iliya Minhas (7)
Central Park Primary School, London

How A Little Sister Is

My little sister is the most cutest,
She won't even go to school,
She feels funny, even when it's sunny,
One time, she ate rice,
And her dolls turn into mice,
She just wants to have a pool.

Rayah Rayah (7)
Central Park Primary School, London

Sarah

S ee me for who I am,
A young girl, free and fair,
R ejoicing in the friends I have,
A life that's gleeful and without a care.
H appy, content, innocent like a lamb.

Sarah Yasmin (6)
Central Park Primary School, London

Monkey

Monkey big and small swinging on a tree
One fell down and hurt her knee
Now the mum called the doctor to come and see
Knowing the silly little monkey hurt her knee
You must stop swinging on the tree.

Anayah Arif (7)
Central Park Primary School, London

Cartoons

C oco is kind
A nd
R eally fun
T oo interesting
O thers can learn
O thers can watch too
N ever stop watching
S nickers is cheeky.

Mukarram Ali Shan (6)
Central Park Primary School, London

My Brother's Tenth Birthday

It's my brother's tenth birthday,
It's going to be a very fun day,
We are celebrating on a Sunday,
Lots of presents and food are ready,
I will give my brother a teddy.

Zarah Zeeshan (7)
Central Park Primary School, London

The Blooming Sky

The beautiful sky
Shines in the night,
Blooming, zooming, glowing,
The birds fly in the sky,
The stars shine so bright,
I see a bright light in the night,
What a sight!

Saad Javed (6)
Central Park Primary School, London

All About Me

I love roses,
I love my mum,
And my hobbies are art, reading and baking,
My favourite colours are red, pink and purple
My passion is writing,
My favourite drink is Vimto.

Arya Choudhury (6)
Central Park Primary School, London

I Love Mermaids!

Mermaids are bright,
And love light,
Mermaids are cool,
And love school,
And they are sweet,
And they meet,
Mermaids are kind,
And use things with their hands.

Jasleen Singh Tena (7)
Central Park Primary School, London

The Bakery

I like the bakery,
But I think it has a mystery.
The bakery has food,
When I visit, I'm in a good mood.
When I go inside,
I look at the menu and can't decide.

Karina Croitoriu (6)
Central Park Primary School, London

All About Friends

F orever together
R eady to help
I mportant to me
E asy to get along with
N ever too busy
D ear to me
S pecial to me.

Halima Alam (7)
Central Park Primary School, London

My Cat

My cat has a hat
And I gave it a pat
But where is my cat?
It flew on a carpet
To the market
And saw a rat
Wearing a hat
Hiding under the mat.

Khadijah Sultan (6)
Central Park Primary School, London

Nutty Cats

C razy cats, they sleep all day
A nd go mad for laser beams
T onight they will go crazy for food
S o let them sleep the next day.

Qaasim Desai (7)
Central Park Primary School, London

Dada And Me

D o you know who he is?
A kind and happy face,
D ada is my best friend,
A nd my hero!

Idris Raja Ali (4)
Central Park Primary School, London

I Am A Brachiosaurus

I am a brachiosaurus,
I like to eat leaves,
I can stomp,
I can roar,
I can smell the trees.

Syed Muhammad Mudassir Shah (6)
Central Park Primary School, London

Big Ben

B ig Ben is big.
I t's in London and I went to Big Ben.
G old and brown.

B ig Ben is cornered by the Houses of Parliament
E very day it chimes and New Year
N o people live here.

Klyan Afrose (6)
Downshall Primary School, Seven Kings

Big Ben

Big Ben is old
At night, people see Big Ben
Big Ben has patterns
I went to see Big Ben
Big Ben had lots of patterns
Every day, people come to see Big Ben
At night, people see Big Ben.

Nimrit Kaur (5)
Downshall Primary School, Seven Kings

Big Ben

B en has a clock in the middle.
I t is Big Ben.
G olden Big Ben.

B ig Ben is in London.
E very hour, hey it chimes.
N ow it is old.

Maryam Aidha (5)
Downshall Primary School, Seven Kings

Big Ben

B ig Ben is tall,
I t's in London,
G old and brown.

B ig Ben has a clock,
E very day, it chimes,
N o people, not allowed.

Ahmad Patel (6)
Downshall Primary School, Seven Kings

Big Ben

B ig Ben is in London,
I t is tall,
G old and brown,

B ig Ben is old,
E very day people see Big Ben,
N o one lives in Big Ben.

Yahya Santally (5)
Downshall Primary School, Seven Kings

Big Ben

B ig Ben is tall.
I went to see Big Ben.
G old and brown.

B ig Ben has a clock.
E very day it chimes.
N obody lives inside.

Imaani Ahmed (5)
Downshall Primary School, Seven Kings

Big Ben

B ig Ben has a clock.
I t is tall.
G old and brown.

B ig Ben is old.
E veryone visits Big Ben.
N o people live in there.

Yafiah Adeel (6)
Downshall Primary School, Seven Kings

Big Ben

B ig Ben is tall.
I went to Big Ben.
G old and silver.

B ig Ben chimes.
E veryone goes to Big Ben.
N ew Year chimes.

Salaar Tayub (6)
Downshall Primary School, Seven Kings

Big Ben

B ig Ben is tall.
I t has a chime.
G o, Big Ben.

B ang, bing, bong
E vening, morning long
N ever stops, the Big Ben.

Nuh Valli (5)
Downshall Primary School, Seven Kings

Big Ben In London

London is loud.
Oh my goodness.
How are you, Queen?
Do you hear Big Ben chime?
On the red bus, I drink water.
Now I am going home.

Miguel Omieczynska-Sipi (6)
Downshall Primary School, Seven Kings

Big Ben

Big Ben is tall,
Big Ben has hands,
Big Ben rings every day,
Big Ben has a clock.

Pranavi Vengatesan (6)
Downshall Primary School, Seven Kings

Transformers

T ransformers change into cars and trucks and all sorts of things
R acecar Transformers have wheels that go very fast
A nd they can also go through portals and teleport to places
N aughty Transformers are called Decepticons
S ome of them can jump really high
F ighting each other for the AllSpark
O ptimus Prime, Megatron and Bumblebee are my favourite Transformers
R escue bots help people and lift them away from danger
M etal makes them super strong so they don't break when they walk
E very Transformer is a different colour

R ed, blue and black are Optimus Prime's colours
S uper strong and good – I love Transformers!

Harrison Pasfield (5)
Edgebury Primary School, Chislehurst

Amazing Animals On Safari

I'm excited to see,
Lots of animals free.
I like seeing zebras with their stripes,
And watching the flamingos take flight.
Elephants are very tall,
Whereas lemurs are very small.
But the animals I like the most,
Are the ones that don't live near the coast.
It's the fierce ones with their roars,
That go speeding on their paws.
I really like the lions, tigers, and leopards,
But you'd better watch out if you're a shepherd!
I'd love to go on safari one day,
It would be an amazing trip away.

Ada Harrison (5)
Edgebury Primary School, Chislehurst

Funny Animals I Can See!

I can see a mouse dancing in a house
I can see a dog scratching a log
I can see a cat wearing a silly hat
I can see a llama wearing a dotty pyjama
I can see a lizard stuck in a blizzard
I can see a mole eating a chocolate roll
I can see ants wearing smelly pants
I can see a bear licking a pear
I can see a snail sitting on a whale
I can see a goat in a pink fluffy coat
I can see a flamingo losing at bingo
I can see a rat flying on a mat
I can see a bee drinking honey tea
I can see a cow doing a big bow!

Harleen Kaur Blaggan (5)
Edgebury Primary School, Chislehurst

Rapunzel And Alice In Wonderland

W edding day!
O n this day, Alice in Wonderland met Rapunzel.
"N ow we need to go to the shops?"
"D ad!" said Rapunzel. "Let's go!"
E lla the dog yapped and went to sleep.
R apunzel, her dad and Alice went home,
L icking ice cream,
A nd Rapunzel had a pop-up lollipop.
"N ot going to the park now, too late,"
D ad said, "Let's have hot chocolate."

Alice Fairhurst-Stanier (4)
Edgebury Primary School, Chislehurst

Penguin Power

P enguins are really playful
E very penguin's got skills and power
N ever kill penguins!
G o and play, my friends
U p and down they go
I nto the water, they hunt their prey
N or do they like grizzly bears

P enguins are really special
O n the ocean they go
W ould they get tired?
E very penguin is different
R yan wants to hug all of them.

Ryan Khosoroshahy (7)
Edgebury Primary School, Chislehurst

Spring

I can hear the tweets of cute, fluffy chicks,
Newly hatched from their eggs.
I can see vivid yellows, pinks and blues
Of daffodils and spring bulbs as they dance in the breeze.
I can smell the fresh green grass
As the roar of the lawnmower fills the air.
I can taste sweet, creamy chocolate
After the Easter bunny hops to visit.
I can feel the warmth of the golden sunshine,
When I look up into the pale blue sky.

Violet Wilcox (7)
Edgebury Primary School, Chislehurst

My School

M y school is a beautiful place to learn,
Y ou and me can make our dreams come true,

S etting the school values in our lives,
C hallenge, opportunity, respect and creativity,
H aving fun and playing while learning every day,
O ut on the green, we do our PE,
O ur teachers and friends, a family so grand,
L et's be safe, not rough, hand in hand.

Jinay Godha (7)
Edgebury Primary School, Chislehurst

Blast-Off Earth

B lack holes suck
L ight.
A stronauts conquer
S pace.
T he first humans

O ff the Earth
F iring their rockets,
F ear nothing, just race.

E ngineering marvels,
A fter the unknown they've flown,
R eaching further and further,
T hen reach their hearts and phone
H ome.

Tomás Da Costa Fonseca (6)
Edgebury Primary School, Chislehurst

Harry Potter Of Gryffindor

H arry is a wizard
A ragog is spooky
R on is a good friend
R avenclaw is blue
Y ule Ball is for dancing.

P rofessor Dumbledore is great
O llivanders is where the magic began
T om Riddle is a villain
T he Whomping Willow catches us in the car
"**E** xpecto Patronum!"
R ead the books.

Ted Power (6)
Edgebury Primary School, Chislehurst

What Am I? Peek-A-Boo!

I have curly, fluffy hair,
Which is white as snow,
I have a very good nose,
For discovering where to go,
I chase my tail when I am very pale,
And I am scared of thunder and hail,
My favourite thing is to chase balls,
I'll ask you to do it more and more,
At the end of the day, I'll cuddle up with you,
Because I love people through and through.

Leila Mustafaj (6)
Edgebury Primary School, Chislehurst

Sparkles The Unicorn

I sparkle and glitter with rainbow-like hair,
I hop and I skip and I fly through the air.
My coat is so shiny it lights up the sky,
With diamonds and jewels that sparkle the eye.
My horn is long and gold and twists like a shell,
With a flick and a swish, it can cast magic spells.
Glitter and sparkles that is my name,
The sparkly unicorn that brightens the day.

Poppy Williams (6)
Edgebury Primary School, Chislehurst

Summer Season

I can see the sun, warm and bright.
I can see the flowers, fresh and light.
I can hear birds chirping, up early for school.
I can hear children splashing in the paddling pool.
I can feel a warm breeze on my nose,
And sand from the beach between my toes.
I can taste delicious ice cream, creamy and sweet.
I can smell cut grass underneath my feet.

Tilly Cheeseman (7)
Edgebury Primary School, Chislehurst

The Dog Goes To School

I can see excited children.
I can hear their laughter.
I can feel their hands stroking my soft fur.
I can smell so many things like perfume, sweets in pockets, flowers in the air and grass on the ground.
I can taste the fresh cool running stream water.
I sense the children's happiness and it makes me happy too.
My day at school was the best.

Finlay Smith (7)
Edgebury Primary School, Chislehurst

Poppy The Penguin

P oppy the penguin has lots of friends,
E veryone wants to play with Poppy because she is really kind,
N o one is sad when Poppy is around,
G reat fun for everyone,
U nder the sea ice, they like to play,
I n Antarctica they catch fish for their lunch,
N ot a chance you will have a bad day with Poppy.

Olive Alcock (6)
Edgebury Primary School, Chislehurst

Allosaurus

I can see an allosaurus.
I can hear its roar!
I can see an allosaurus.
I can feel its rough, scaly skin.
I can see an allosaurus.
I can taste the camptosaurus and stegosaurus from far away.
I can see an allosaurus.
I can smell meat.
When I sense an allosaurus
I run away and scream, "I'm not meat!"

Alex Lintern (6)
Edgebury Primary School, Chislehurst

Kicking A Ball

Running down the pitch,
And feeling the nice breeze,
Everyone cheers,
And I hear them when I score a goal,
I can see a big gap to run in,
So my teammate can pass to me,
I can taste victory
I am going to win the World Cup,
I fell into the smelliest mud,
Because the other team tackled me!

Nason Taylor-Holmes (7)
Edgebury Primary School, Chislehurst

Football Stadium

Football stadium, it's like a big city.
Football stadium, it sounds like birds singing but way louder.
Football stadium, it makes me feel happy when I score a goal.
Football stadium, it makes me feel like Chelsea scoring a goal.
Football stadium, it makes me think of the colour blue because Chelsea is blue.

Lucas Halley (6)
Edgebury Primary School, Chislehurst

Crazy About Unicorns

U nder the sky, over the clouds,
N ever to be seen but always believed,
I n your dreams, forever and ever,
C hasing rainbows,
O ver the sky, flying high,
R ainbow colours and white tails,
N ight-time is when they sleep,
S ugar is what they eat.

Milan D'Rozario (5)
Edgebury Primary School, Chislehurst

The Elf, The Unicorn And The Mermaid

The elf sat on the shelf
He jumped up high and touched the sky
He fell down on his knees
The unicorn sat on the lawn
She jumped up high and touched the sky
Then jumped on the trampoline
The mermaid sat in the shade
She jumped up high and touched the sky
Then splashed all her friends.

Lydia Mathieson (4)
Edgebury Primary School, Chislehurst

Poemasaurus

D anger everywhere.
I am terrified.
N oises of loud dinosaurs.
O h no, a dinosaur!
S -s-spinosaurus is coming this way
A argh, run!
U p there, a pteranodon.
R oar! Tyrannosaurus rex chases the stegosaurus away.
S afe at last.

Louis Burtt (7)
Edgebury Primary School, Chislehurst

Beach Days

I can see gleeful children playing in the splashing waves.
I can hear the squawking seagulls dipping down to the sparkly sea.
I can feel the golden sand between my toes, and the scorching sun on my nose.
I can smell sizzling sausages on the barbecue.
I can taste the sweet ice cream cooling me down.

Senan Harris (6)
Edgebury Primary School, Chislehurst

Spring Delight

I can see the brown, yellow and red leaves fall off the big chunky tree.
I can hear the wind flowing in the big, blue sky.
I can feel the soft, harmless air blowing in my face.
I can taste the yummy, appetising, delightful and delicious chocolate eggs.
I can smell the green, fresh lawn.

George Celaschi (6)
Edgebury Primary School, Chislehurst

Winter

I can see the fluffy, white snowballs falling from the sky.
I can hear shiny teeth shivering and shaking in the cold.
I can feel my fuzzy, cosy coat warming me up.
I can taste warm hot chocolate with squishy marshmallows.
I can smell warm, tasty chicken to warm people up.

Melisa Mehmet (7)
Edgebury Primary School, Chislehurst

Edgebury

E dgebury rocks!
D iamond is my class,
G oing out to play,
E ating in the lunch hall,
B asketball hoops for playing,
U niform is red and white and grey,
R ed bus for reading,
Y ou will love my class.

Jaxon Davis (5)
Edgebury Primary School, Chislehurst

The Fruit Is Good

F ruit is a very good snack,
R emember to put some in your rucksack,
U nless you don't like sour,
I suggest you eat an orange every twenty-four hours,
T here are fruits for every taste,
S urely none will go to waste!

Nora Marini (7)
Edgebury Primary School, Chislehurst

Seaside Winter Walk

I can see huge waves crashing against the sea wall
I can hear the huge white seagulls trying to eat my chips
I can feel the huge gusts of wind on my face
I can taste the salty sea spray on my tongue
I can smell yummy hot chocolate coming from the harbour cafe.

Maddie Sharps (7)
Edgebury Primary School, Chislehurst

Cake

Cake is sweet to eat
Towers of icing, nice and neat
Cream in the middle, forming soft sheets
Making each slice delicious to eat
Cakes for every occasion, no matter how big or small
But cakes with sprinkles and glitter are the best of them all.

Bethany Da Silva (7)
Edgebury Primary School, Chislehurst

Football Poem

F ootball is fun
O ver the goal
O ffside, says the referee
T he score is 6-5
B alls are flying everywhere
A t the pitch, we play
L et's try to score more
L osing is never fun!

Jacob Borg (6)
Edgebury Primary School, Chislehurst

Dinosaurs On A Rainbow Bus

R aaa
A dinosaur said
I n the bus
N ice dinosaurs on the
B us
O n the bus
W as a tiger

B us full of dinosaurs
U p the hill
S top! This is our stop.

Alex Foster (4)
Edgebury Primary School, Chislehurst

Walking In The Summer

I can see the burning yellow sun heating me up
I can feel the green, long grass brushing along my feet
I can smell the colourful nice flowers
I can hear the black and yellow bees buzzing
I can taste the cold ice cream I am eating as I walk.

Leo Gooding (7)
Edgebury Primary School, Chislehurst

Magical Land

I have a unicorn,
I am a unicorn,

I like rainbows, they are magic,
I have magical horns,
They make rainbows,
I feel happy when I'm with my friends,
I love to make shows,
Where I sing,
I am a unicorn.

Isabelle Naden (6)
Edgebury Primary School, Chislehurst

Kipper The Cat

Kipper the cat, you are so furry and fluffy.
Kipper the cat, I can hear you purring.
Kipper the cat, you are very big.
Kipper the cat, your dinner smells a bit fishy.
Kipper the cat, you are so cute, I just want to cuddle you.

Emelia Harris (6)
Edgebury Primary School, Chislehurst

Percy Hamster

P ercy is a hamster, all chubby and fluffy,
E verybody loves him, especially me,
R ound cheeks always filled with food,
C hewing tubes puts him in a good mood,
Y ou are the best pet in the world!

Ophelia Nelson (5)
Edgebury Primary School, Chislehurst

Spring

S un is hot when it is spring
P urple flower's name is lavender
R oses have a lovely smell
I love spring when it's hot
N ice flowers smell good
G ood flowers look nice.

Joshua Banis (6)
Edgebury Primary School, Chislehurst

My Furry Friend

I can see your lovely cosy fur,
I can hear your heartbeat when I cuddle you closely,
I can feel your wet tongue when you lick me,
I can taste your excitement when I come home from school,
I can smell your dog biscuits.

Annie Manning (6)
Edgebury Primary School, Chislehurst

Strong

S un is shining
T he sun brightly shines up in the blue sky
R unning around for all to see
O n a good day
N othing will keep me away
G etting stronger and stronger.

Alisa Bejan (5)
Edgebury Primary School, Chislehurst

Rainbow Sugar Glide

I can see a lovely bright unicorn,
I can hear a horsey sound, *clip-clop*.
I can feel the rainbow sparkly mane,
I can taste the magical unicorn food.
I can smell delicious rainbow magic in the sky.

Nina Vaccarino (6)
Edgebury Primary School, Chislehurst

Summertime

I can see flowers,
Blooming in the field,
I can hear birds singing in the trees,
I can feel the wind blowing in my hair,
I can taste sweet strawberries,
I can smell sunflowers in the fresh grass.

Emre Azmi (6)
Edgebury Primary School, Chislehurst

Kick Football

Black and white rolls across the grass,
The crowd cheers loudly,
I feel hot because I run a lot,
I can taste sweat and it is salty,
The smell of mud and grass fills my nose,
I love football.

Austin Haines (6)
Edgebury Primary School, Chislehurst

Diamond

D iamond rocks
I love Diamond class
A ll of us have fun
M e and my friends work
O n the same team
N o one gives up
D iamonds are the best.

Amanie Clement (6)
Edgebury Primary School, Chislehurst

Puppies

I can see very well so I can see very far away,
I can hear things with my floppy ears,
I can feel soft grass underneath my paws,
I can taste dry dog food in my mouth,
I can smell dog bums.

Halle Exford Downes (7)
Edgebury Primary School, Chislehurst

Monkeys

M onkeys like bananas
O ver the trees, they go
N ever hurt monkeys
K eep looking after them
E very monkey is important
Y ay! Monkeys are the best!

Chester Ramsden (6)
Edgebury Primary School, Chislehurst

Little Unicorn

I love unicorns very much,
They are living in Wonderland,
I love unicorns every day,
Maybe they come for dinner today!
I love unicorns, yes I do,
I like to have one,
You too?

Neli Roslaniec (4)
Edgebury Primary School, Chislehurst

My Senses Poem

I can see a beautiful sandy beach.
I can hear some fluttering butterflies.
I can feel bright sunshine, hot on my skin.
I can taste a yummy ice cream.
I can smell the salty sea air.

Saraya Matharu (7)
Edgebury Primary School, Chislehurst

Sparkles

S hiny and beautiful
P erfectly bright
A mazing
R eally colourful
K een to see the
L ights
E very day
S pectacular!

Noelle De Chavez (5)
Edgebury Primary School, Chislehurst

Fairy

F ast asleep in my bed,
A dummy fairy came,
I saw her magic sparkle and glow,
R eally hope she's brought my watch,
Y es, I am a big girl now!

Freja Warren (4)
Edgebury Primary School, Chislehurst

Winter

W inter is very cold,
I ce skating is fun,
N umbing my hands and feet,
T rees have no leaves,
E xcited kids,
R eady to build a snowman.

Giuseppe Noto (6)
Edgebury Primary School, Chislehurst

Zara

Z ara is good
A lways listening
R ides a bike at weekends
A sks lots of questions.

H elps Daddy tidy up
W atches funny films.

Zara Hersey-Walker (6)
Edgebury Primary School, Chislehurst

My Mummy

M y mummy is the best
U nique, special and funny
M ummy gives me cuddles
M y mummy always has good ideas
Y ou are the best and I love you.

James Munro (5)
Edgebury Primary School, Chislehurst

Poppy

P oppy is my dog,
O h, I love her so much!
P oppy's ears are floppy,
P ops is her name for short,
Y ou will love her as much as me.

Lily-Grace Eaves (5)
Edgebury Primary School, Chislehurst

Space

S pace is big and has eight planets
P lanets are made of rock
A stronauts can visit space
C omets are big icy rocks
E arth is our home.

Zac Kenny (6)
Edgebury Primary School, Chislehurst

A Cold Riddle

I am found in winter
I fall from the sky
I am made out of water
Sometimes you can play with me
I can be thick or thin

What am I?

I am snow.

Cyrus Phan (6)
Edgebury Primary School, Chislehurst

Spring

S unny walks
P icnics in the park
R abbits hopping
I ce cream cones
N ice days to play outside
G reen grass and flowers.

Luca Wall (5)
Edgebury Primary School, Chislehurst

Little Ladybird

L ittle legs
A nd
D ark eyes.
Y our favourite insect.
B lack spots
I n a
R ed body.
D rifting by.

Iris Haines (4)
Edgebury Primary School, Chislehurst

Apple Tree

I can see my apple tree
I can hear it blowing in the wind
I can feel the apples growing
I can taste the apple fruit
I can smell apple blossom.

Desara Brahaj (6)
Edgebury Primary School, Chislehurst

Flower

E very flower is different,
S ome flowers are tall and some are short,
M any flowers have nectar,
E very flower has petals.

Esme Pfeiffer (6)
Edgebury Primary School, Chislehurst

Summer Sun

I can see the blue sky.
I can hear the birds fly.
I can feel the warmest heart.
I can taste ice cream so sweet.
I can smell the air so fresh.

Arian Jeddi (6)
Edgebury Primary School, Chislehurst

My Family

I see my brother playing,
I smell my mummy's tea,
I taste my mama's food,
I feel my nana's cuddles,
I hear my family chatting.

Olivia Rorison-Warburton (6)
Edgebury Primary School, Chislehurst

My Powers

E mily is great,
M y powers are good to write,
I am good at being kind,
L ove children,
Y ou are great.

Emily Watts Stropute (5)
Edgebury Primary School, Chislehurst

Trains

T rains are fast,
R ails are shiny,
A mazing journeys,
I am on a train,
N othing is better than trains.

Liam Carta (6)
Edgebury Primary School, Chislehurst

Puffy Poem

Puffy, Puffy, I'm glad you are here.
He has been here nearly a year.
We love your ways.
We love your plays.
Please will you stay?

Cody Carey (7)
Edgebury Primary School, Chislehurst

Maeve

Flowers are made from seeds,
Flowers grow from the root,
Flowers have petals,
Flowers are planted in the garden,
Flowers are spring!

Freya Putz (5)
Edgebury Primary School, Chislehurst

Portugal

I can see Ronaldo
I can hear the fans
I can feel the green grass
I can taste my hot dog while I watch the game
I can smell victory.

George Pinker (6)
Edgebury Primary School, Chislehurst

Sweet Pete

A boy called Pete ate lots of sweets
And had big feet
He was nice to meet
He had to wear big shoes
And he liked to watch the news

Lyla Jaques (7)
Edgebury Primary School, Chislehurst

My Senses Poem

I can see bright yellow sunshine
I can hear trains
I can feel a warm, soft coat
I can taste the apple
I can smell the dirt.

Dealarra Ezzra Muhd Azrainuddin (6)
Edgebury Primary School, Chislehurst

What Am I?

I swim in the Arctic
I have a long tusk
You can call it a tooth
I am the unicorn of the sea
No animal is as elegant as me.

Zahara Okasha (6)
Edgebury Primary School, Chislehurst

Smile

Things that make me

- **S** pider-Man
- **M** y family
- **I** ce cream
- **L** ego
- **E** xploring.

Ari Aubeeluck (5)
Edgebury Primary School, Chislehurst

I See What I See

When I look in the mirror
I see someone who looks familiar
Hello, I say, do I know you?
Yes, it's my friend Eliza.

Eliza Gregoriou (6)
Edgebury Primary School, Chislehurst

Cats

C ats are my favourite,
A mazing colours,
T hey love yawn,
S ometimes they like to snuggle.

Ela Nacar (6)
Edgebury Primary School, Chislehurst

Some Things I Like

S uper cool,
I ce cream,
D ancing dude,
N ature,
E arth,
Y oghurt.

Sidney Hayes (6)
Edgebury Primary School, Chislehurst

My Five Senses

I see with my eyes.
I hear with my ears.
I taste with my mouth.
I smell with my nose.
I feel with my skin.

Anthony Woodward (4)
Edgebury Primary School, Chislehurst

Robots

Robots are made of metal,
Dobots are made of dough.
Bobots are made of bows
And snowbots are made of snow.

Amos Reynolds (5)
Edgebury Primary School, Chislehurst

I Am A Dog

I am a dog,
I see a park,
I hear a bark,
I taste a treat,
I smell your feet,
I feel the grass.

Quincy Rawlings (5)
Edgebury Primary School, Chislehurst

Pretty Kitty Cat

Paws, purr, fur, meow
Sleeping
Running
Hiding
Whiskers, ears, eyes, tail
Pretty kitty cat.

Amelia Reid (4)
Edgebury Primary School, Chislehurst

Tomato Soup

I look red.
I smell nice.
I feel wet, sticky and hot.
I taste yummy.
I hear a bubbly sound.

Eldridge Ofori-Boakye (6)
Edgebury Primary School, Chislehurst

Finn

F unny and friendly
I s always happy
N ever naughty and
N ever gives up.

Finn Thomas (5)
Edgebury Primary School, Chislehurst

The C Sound

Cat goes *meow*
Car goes *brrrm*
Cake yummy
Carrots yuck
Cunning plan, hmm.

Freddie Dykes (4)
Edgebury Primary School, Chislehurst

Santa Flies

S anta flies,
A t,
N ight,
T o deliver,
A ll the presents.

Finley Borg (4)
Edgebury Primary School, Chislehurst

Ruby

R uby is my dog
U nder the table
B itey
Y ou are the best puppy.

Jake Manning (4)
Edgebury Primary School, Chislehurst

The Bus To School

The bus has arrived
All get on board
We are going to school
To learn a lot.

Lum Iberhasaj (6)
Edgebury Primary School, Chislehurst

Cat

C ats sit on mats
A nd they are fluffy
T ickle their tummies.

Joseph Clement (4)
Edgebury Primary School, Chislehurst

Snow

S now is cold
N ot hot
O n roofs
W hite.

Leila Francis (5)
Edgebury Primary School, Chislehurst

Night Sky

The stars are glowing
Like a light
High up in the night
Sky.

Ronnie Whitlock (5)
Edgebury Primary School, Chislehurst

Archie

I am a statue,
Still and sparkly,
And my name is Archie.

Archie Whitlock (4)
Edgebury Primary School, Chislehurst

Spider-Man

My best hero is Spider-Man,
Who can be like him?
I can!

Jacob Rudnicki (5)
Edgebury Primary School, Chislehurst

Cats And Bats

Cats,
Bats,
What are bats?
They are tiny cats.

Mila Xhetani (7)
Edgebury Primary School, Chislehurst

Cat

C ute eyes,
A te mice,
T wice!

Isla Turner (4)
Edgebury Primary School, Chislehurst

YOUNG WRITERS INFORMATION

We hope you have enjoyed reading this book – and that you will continue to in the coming years.

If you're the parent or family member of an enthusiastic poet or story writer, do visit our website www.youngwriters.co.uk/subscribe and sign up to receive news, competitions, writing challenges and tips, activities and much, much more! There's lots to keep budding writers motivated!

If you would like to order further copies of this book, or any of our other titles, then please give us a call or order via your online account.

Young Writers
Remus House
Coltsfoot Drive
Peterborough
PE2 9BF
(01733) 890066
info@youngwriters.co.uk

Join in the conversation!
Tips, news, giveaways and much more!

YoungWritersUK YoungWritersCW
youngwriterscw youngwriterscw